THIS BOOK BELONGS TO:

_____

Dedicated to all the astrology lovers.

All rights reserved.
No part of this book may be reproduced in any form or by any means, electronic or mechanical, and no photocopying or recording, unless you have written permission from the author.

ISBN 978-1-958985-42-7

Text copyright © 2025 by Mimi Jones

www.joeysavestheday.com

A Mimi Book

WELCOME TO: THE WONDERFUL WORLD OF ZODIACS

ARIES

Mimi Jones

Ruling Planet:

Mars is the planet that rules Aries.

ADVENTURE awaits

Personality:
Aries are adventurous and love trying new things.

LEADER

Strength:

They are natural leaders and love taking charge.

IMPATIENT

Weakness:

Aries can be a bit impatient.

Color:

Red is their lucky color.

Aries

Lucky Numbers:

1, 8, and 17 are lucky numbers for Aries.

1 8 17

Lucky

Compatibility:

Aries gets along well with Leo, Sagittarius, Gemini, and Aquarius.

LEO

AQUARIUS

GEMINI

SAGITTARIUS

Dislikes:

They don't like waiting or being bored.

ARIES

Loading...

Likes:

Aries loves physical challenges and sports.

LEADER

Career:

They do well in jobs where they can lead and compete.

Negative Trait:

Sometimes, Aries can be a bit too aggressive.

Motto:

The motto of Aries is "I am."

I am enough

Favorite Days:

Tuesday and Saturday are their most favorable days.

tuesday

&

saturday

Health:
Aries should take care of their head.

Famous Aries:

Famous Aries include Vincent van Gogh, Reese Witherspoon, and Mariah Carey.

Style:

They like bold and confident styles, often wearing red.

Challenges:
Aries needs to learn patience.

Patience is a **VIRTUE**

Love Life:
In relationships, Aries are passionate and honest.

honest

LOVE

Favorite Activities:

Aries loves adventures and new experiences.

The **ADVENTURE** begins

Symbolic Animal:
The Ram represents their strength and determination.

If you liked this Zodiac book. Check out my other Zodiac books here:

www.mimibooks.com

THE END!

www.ingramcontent.com/pod-product-compliance
Lightning Source LLC
Chambersburg PA
CBHW042132070426
42453CB00002BA/72